TOLU AND THE ANTELOPE!

This storybook "TOLU AND THE ANTELOPE" tells an amazing story about a little boy and his wonderful antelope.

The storybook creates emotional bonds between children and pets and helps them develop basic language skills and profoundly expand their vocabularies.

The book also demonstrates an awareness of children's own environment and well-being.

In addition, it encourages early literacy in children.

TOLU AND THE
PAINTING ANTELOPE
BY: SHOLA AJASA

ISBN: 9798363257063

This book is dedicated to my children.

CONTENTS

CHAPTER 1

Once upon a time, there was a small town called **Farmville.**

In Farmville, there are so many places to visit.

There are farms, museums, shopping malls, schools, hospitals, animal zoos, lakes, and rivers.

A little boy named Tolu lives in the town of Farmville.

Tolu was an inspiring painter.

He likes to paint during the weekends on Saturdays and Sundays.

CHAPTER 2

Tolu's Farm.

Tolu also likes to visit his family's farm, outside the town.

Tolu likes to play with some of the animals on their farms such as pigs, cows, chickens, goats, puppies, and antelope.

The animals also like to play with Tolu. They were always looking forward to playing with him on Saturdays and Sundays when there are no schools.

The animals will scream whenever they see Tolu arriving at the farm. The goat will scream meh-eh-eh! The puppies will start swinging their tails, the chickens will start following him around, …. shouting crock, crock … and the antelope will be jumping and dancing toward Tolu – singing meeeeeeeeeh.

Chapter 3

Favourite animal.

Tolu's favourite animal is the antelope!

Tolu always buys clothes and gifts for his antelope!

One day, there was so much rain that some parts of the farm were flooded, and his antelope was feeling cold.

Tolu wraps his antelope with a cloth immediately because he was feeling cold.

The antelope was very happy with Tolu, and he stood up on his feet to say "*thank you Tolu*" – I feel very warm now!

Chapter 4

Cool idea!

Tolu always likes to paint whenever there are no schools or when he is feeling bored at home or on the farm.

He likes to paint his favourite antelope and bought paint brush, board, different paint colours, etc. He loves to paint his other animals too.

Tolu decided that one day he would teach his antelope how to paint.

He thought it would be cool for his antelope to draw other animals. He was so happy with his new ideas!

Chapter 5

Rainstorm!

One day, on a Sunday evening, there was a rainstorm that flooded the main city including his school. It affected his animal shelter too as they become homeless.

Tolu's father told him It will take seven days for the repairs in the school to be done.

Some of the trees and power lines were down too.

Tolu thought about what to do during these seven days.
He doesn't want to be very bored at home. He decided on a plan of what to do from Monday to Saturday!

CHAPTER 6

Monday & Tuesday!

Tolu decided it would be fun with his paintings and will teach his antelope how to paint on Monday and Tuesday.

He bought another set of canvas, paints, brushes, etc., and started teaching his antelope how to paint on their farm, very close to the riverside.

Tolu was so happy in the afternoon, on Tuesday, to see his antelope standing and painting beside him.

CHAPTER 7

Wednesday!

Tolu went to the farm on Wednesday to feed his animal friends.

He gave them lots of animal treats, grasses, and milk for the goat and his antelope to make them healthy.

His animals looked up at him and said to him "thank you Tolu" for giving us food.

Food

CHAPTER 8

Thursday!

Tolu decided to paint flowers on Thursday because
there was no school and he doesn't want to get bored.

Tolu brought his canvas, brushes, and paints to the farm and draw two beautiful trees and three flowers.

He showed his animal friends and his favourite antelope, and he was very happy.

CHAPTER 9

Friday!

On Friday morning, Tolu woke up and started thinking about why the power lines were down.

So, Tolu went to the riverbank to get new inspiration about electricity.

He thought to himself about other ways to generate electricity such as solar, wind turbines, etc.

CHAPTER 10

Saturday!

On Saturday, Tolu decided to take his antelope for swimming in the river.

He quickly wraps his antelope in clothes when his friend was feeling cold after swimming.

His antelope looked up at him and said "thank you Tolu" for keeping me warm.

CHAPTER 11

Sunday!

On Sunday morning, Tolu went to see his animal friends at the farm and was very surprised at what he saw.

Whaaooah, he saw his antelope standing and painting other animal friends on the canvas. His antelope was holding the brush in his mouth and painting beautiful pictures!

The cow was really surprised too! The cow shouted "Moooooo" - you're good antelope! The Antelope painted Chickens and goats too and they all love his paintings.
This gesture from the antelope leads to the cow and the rest of the farm animal painting each other on a canvas.

On Sunday evening, Tolu decided to do another painting before the school opens on the next day, Monday.

Finally, Tolu painted the blue colours of the river, and he was so happy with all his paintings.

ACTIVITY PAGE

After reading the book, educators can encourage students to write letters to an animal shelter to know more about their needs and how students can help.

Other activities could be:

- Field trip to an animal shelter in the community
- Ask students about their favourite animals (what's your favourite animal)
- Field trip to see the animal farm/ where food has been grown
- Ask kids about their favourite place in their community
- Survey pages (favourite animal, favourite places in the community, favourite fruits) tabular form of surveys
- Counts how many people, and animals in the story
- Ask about the setting of the story
- Favourite part of the setting
- Encourage students to tell the beginning, middle, and end of the story
- Their favourite part of the story and why, etc.

Shola Ajasa is a highly respected and knowledgeable Early Childhood Educationist. She has over a decade of facilitating learning with children and those with special needs in Ontario, Canada. She has published a series of educational books for early childhood learning. Among her books in recent years are *"Knock, Knock, who is there"*, *"Sometimes, I feel like…"*, **"Tidy Up Your Mess"**, and *"Kinder Rockstar"*, etc.

This book "**Tolu and His Antelope**" creates awareness for children to foster a good relationship with animals, pets, and other friends thereby enhancing their social emotions and self-regulate.

It also helps children to demonstrate awareness of their own environment and well-being.

.